THE THIRD PERSON

To Alison & Shaun
must be kept
together

Henry x

Henry Normal

INTRODUCTION

This is the sixth in a series of books. Most of the pieces were written between September 1992 and February 1993.

DEDICATED TO WARREN LAKIN

All pieces by HENRY NORMAL.

Cover by EMMA DAMON.

PUBLISHED BY: A. K. PRESS
22 LUTTON PLACE
EDINBURGH
EH8 9PE

PRINTED IN GREAT BRITAIN BY UNICORN PRESS, SHEFFIELD.

CONTENTS

1. The Truth Fairy.
2. The ulterior motivator.
3. Love Ethic.
5. The poem within you.
6. Natasia.
   Love conquers all.
   246414.
7. Sex and the kissing of salt.
8. Nature poem.
   Green Poem.
   Tadpole Family.
9. The sacrement of compost.
10. A baby Magpie.
11. Cardigans to Iraq.
12. Third World War Poems.
13. Skeleton.
14. The third person.
15. The whole woman.
16. Ode to the Trevi fountain surrounded by scaffold;
    The Genius of Michelangelo.
    Titian a bag.
17. Plain Biscuits.
18. Euro Vegas.
19. Open graves.
20. The church of England riots.
21. Hymn of the Madonna's Hymen.
22. An Englishman in New York.
    The World Trade Centre.
    Chelsea Hotel.
    Lincoln Memorial.
23. The nearly famous.
24. Jesus flies business class.
    Sagrada Familia (the Sacred Family).
    Columbus.
25. The uncommon touch.
27. Ten ways to end a relationship.

Cont'd

28. Beyond mathematics.
29. Why I'm against Christmas, New Year, Birthdays and weekends.
30. DB16.
31. In defence of the moustache.
32. The enchantment of personality.
33. The advantages of having your own hand as a sexual partner.
34. Blinking.
35. She has given of herself.
36. Socks appeal.
37. Demoting cupid to a chat show host.
38. The corner of Sackville Street.
39. On stepping out the door all past autumns inhaled.
40. The binary code of existence.
41. Earlobes.
42. Trust me I'm a poet.
43. Tomorrow's worms.
44. Chapel of the metal shroud.
45. Fossils on computer.
46. Recoiling from the anticlimax.

THE THIRD PERSON

THE TRUTH FAIRY

She loves me, she loves me not
Eternity comes and goes as easy as that
Like the crossing of the equator
or the passing of infection

There is something, then there is nothing
and somewhere in-between
there is change

Blood rushes from the heart to the head
and back to the heart
once, twice
and somewhere on its journey back
or it's journey out again
there is change

Breath enters the lungs and
is expelled
once, twice
and somewhere between the expulsion
and the intake of fresh air
there is change

Sensation excites the nerves
a million reactions a second
the pupils dilate and retract
pores react to temperature
yet even without perceived movement
time passes
and there is change

Images illustrate the mind
sometimes erratic, sometimes fluid
conscious and subconscious
some casual
some revealing deliberation
the world outside is as yet unaltered
but there is change

THE ULTERIOR MOTIVATOR

I've looked for you
all my adult life

in the proudest of my achievements
in the embarrassment of my shortcomings
in the possibilities of every relationship
in the eye contact of every stranger

in the opening of every door
from the window of every train
on every horizon out to sea

in loud and smoke filled rooms
over the rim of every glass
across every public gathering
down the line of every queue

in the glare of every headlight
in every face of every crowd

in the most bleak of landscapes
in the closing of every curtain
I've looked for you

LOVE ETHIC

I've brought you some flowers
I hope you like them

I'm not always so forward on a first date
but I've brought you this as well
I hope you don't mind that I've not wrapped it up
It's an album of photos
showing each of my previous lovers
naked
in bed with me
in various positions
taken at the moment of orgasm
with accompanying audio tapes
and videos of the more recent lovers

And then there's all my family photos
A full itinerary of my life so far
A book of my own quotations
A list of all my friends
their likes and dislikes
and a list of their friends

A twelve volume history of my ancestry
The stuffed corpses of all my dead relatives
and life size wax models
of everyone I've ever met
A report from my doctor
My latest X-rays

All the sperm I've ever produced
stretching back to the beginnings of puberty
and all the urine and faeces I've passed

All the hair cut or shaved from my body
my entire collection of toe nail clippings
and the pus squeezed from every boil or spot

All the stale sweat released from my pores

A recent study of my philosophical beliefs
My bank statement
A list of my assets, property
and personal possessions
A detailed career plan for the rest of my life
My star chart
A graph of my biorythms
A signed photo of my God
An explanation of every conscious
or subconscious thought
I've had since my conception
A written declaration of
my expectations in the event of a relationship
An extensive analysis of
all the things we have in common
A list of questions you may want to ask
together with all possible answers

And finally an itemised account as to
how since its creation
the universe
has brought us to this point

I don't suppose you were expecting flowers

THE POEM WITHIN YOU

Opened to the coldness of the room
Is the poem deep inside you
You shrug and feign dismissal
But it is as you'd hoped
It is your poem
Private and sacred
It belongs to you alone
Guarded and enshrined
It is the very heart of you
You are concerned for its progress
You are both embarrassed and proud
And in an act of defiance
In an act of pure humanity
You hold out your poem
Sure that it has it's place
Opened to the coldness of the room
Is the poem deep inside you
And for a moment the room is warmed
And in that moment you are content
And in a world of such poems
How can anyone die lonely and cold?

NATASIA

I loved Natasia
after a fashion
and she could have love me truly
if only after
a night of passion
I hadn't called her Julie

LOVE CONQUERS ALL (a love poem for dyslexics)

B you're adorable
M you're so beautiful
H you're as cute as can be
I may be dyslexic
but I'll try to spell it out
I lob yup

246414

When the phone stops ringing in the other room
of all the people on Earth
I think of you

SEX AND THE KISSING OF SALT

The rhapsody of gesture
a covenant of nature

a merging of fluids and gentleness
the homage of caress
Art at its purest

the warmest gift
a mutual worship

the applauding of skin
the salutation within

the sincerest poetry
the perfect society

the reverence of the body's grace
the innermost embrace

the enchantment of response
the harmony of imbalance

the threshold of adoration
a chemical elation
the theatre of captivation

a more intimate fame
the empathy bargain

the highest courtesy
the noblest chivalry
modesty's brave amnesty

the exaltation of the senses
the camaraderie of indulgences

the ballad of creation
the divine celebration
the glory of immersion

NATURE POEM

Sex in the woods
is a lot of fun
if you don't mind the bugs
and twigs up your bum

GREEN POEM

Green are the English pastures
Green – the jealousy of lovers
Green are the fruit pastels
I always offer to others

TADPOLE FAMILY (In response to Whale Nation by Heathcote Williams)

It's difficult to catch those tadpoles
cos they slip out the net through the holes
but when newly born
they're frog spawn
and that stuff you can scoop up in bowls

THE SACRAMENT OF COMPOST

We are the ripeness of fruit
And the concentration of coal
The eagle and the bear
The Zulu and the Navaho

We are the acids
And the spoor
The amoeba
And the dinosaur
Our common ancestor
The possibility of nature

All flesh is eaten
All blood sipped

Evolution is the Eucharist

We are between
All that was
And all that will
Live

The miracle of the atom
    smacks the breath
        of the dead
            into the child
As life begats life
Begats life

A BABY MAGPIE

All infants have the charm of innocence
untainted by the superstition of experience

yet here only a few days old
an omen to all who behold
in moments of solitude that follow
does this life even now herald
a little sorrow

CARDIGANS TO IRAQ

I have a dream
of a world without armies
A world of peace
where everyone wears cardies

Attack is ONLY the best defence
for those who lack sartorial elegance
It creates an impression to lessen aggression

Hooligans with lager cans
are never dressed in cardigans
Dr Who in his Tardis
was never invaded by Daleks in cardies
You never see a pit bull
in a nice bit of wool
Attila the Hun
never wore a cardigun
The Marquis de Sade he
never wore a cardy
Vinny Jones wouldn't be such a hard man
if he had to play in a cardigan

Better than a sweater or a bullet proof vest
you never see a cardy in battle dress

The UN troops would make proper guardians
If they swopped their berets for light blue cardigans

This paragon of haute couture
could ensure an end to war
So strengthen your defences
with Marks and Spencers

I have a dream on behalf of man
where the symbol of peace and love
is a white dove
in a cardigan

THIRD WORLD WAR POEMS

1. To show how easy it is for a mistake to happen.

Hickory Dickory Dock
The mouse ran up the clock
the clock struck one
causing a pre-emptive strike escalating
into all out nuclear attack
Hickory Dickory Dock

2. About weapons falling into the wrong hands

Mary had a little lamb
She also had a thermo nuclear device
the Armageddon activity set
new from Fisher Price

3. Class comment

Humpty Dumpty sat on a wall
Humpty Dumpty had a great fall
All the King's horses and all the King's men
were safely tucked away in underground bunkers

4. About the affects of nuclear fallout

Mary Mary quite contrary
how does your garden grow?
It doesn't

5. In a similar vein

I had a little pear tree
and nothing would it bear

SKELETON

My teeth are somewhat corroded by sugar
but otherwise despite my figure
My skeleton is not dissimilar to yours

My muscles are weak and wasted
and through lack of use have degenerated
but these will rot long before my bones

My stomach and my legs are swollen
my neck and jowls have become misshapen
All this will disappear as we grow nearer

The soothing of elasticity has deserted my face
my eyes have lost focus with age
soon my hair will begin to skulk away

There is a scent and a texture to my skin
that has at times been found attractive
This will quickly lose its lustre

Personality is demonstrated with each single move
from grace to tragic ineptitude
but inanimate, history will spar with others

Through my conscious fears and aspirations
I unfold my dreams and passions
but with the failing of light
my body will fall derelict

And in 1000 years time, outlasing it all
in a museum or some lecture hall
the scaffold of my core
May well hang side by side with yours
with labels almost identical

THE THIRD PERSON

Using we instead of I
we generalize
and rationalize to anaesthetize
from the emote to the remote
in the you and the he
in the they and the she

we no longer enjoy we appreciate
we no longer experience we spectate

bureaucrats of passion
we diffuse in logic
we dissipate in the analytic

we no longer feel but relate
we no longer talk we discuss
we no longer argue we debate
we no longer react we equate

we dilute to nullify
from the nib to the cursor
as we distance ourselves
in the third person

THE WHOLE WOMAN

I have seen the Venus DeMilo
and she is beautiful
and she spoke with such humanity
I was ashamed

For I had judged her purely on appearance
but not as you might think

I had found her body alluring
and it's poise sensual
but selfish to my perceived boundaries
sensitivity I had shortchanged for lust

Her arms, although this may seem callous
were to me, irrelevant
Were they to be covering her modesty
or spread like a crucifix
beckoning like a lover
or hid away in submission
   In my naivety I am diminished by glib acceptance
   Smarting from my own scars I am left wanting
For then she spoke
and her voice was brave and true
and the figure became flesh
and the body became tender
and the whole woman was revealed
greater than the subtraction of parts
greater than my tourist imagination
could envisage

And as her words seduced my spirit
I was ashamed
how shallow had I been to accept
any less

I have seen the Venus DeMilo
and she has spoken to me
and she is beautiful

ODE TO THE TREVI FOUNTAIN SURROUNDED BY SCAFFOLD

Love sick I maybe
Vino makes me maudlin
but even I couldn't write a song called
3 coins on tarpaulin

THE GENIUS OF MICHELANGELO

When sculpting 'the perfect man'
the real insight of the job
was making 'David's' head too big
in proportion to the size of his nob

TITIAN A BAG

If Titian was painting today
think of the money he'd make
by painting his nudes reclining
eating a Cadbury's flake

PLAIN BISCUITS

Why do rich people insist it's
posh to eat plain biscuits

It seems to me Rich Tea
are for the miserly
and Nice are not nice at any price

Shortbread I particularly dread
I'd sooner have a Happy Face instead

Tradition is fine for old codgers
but the young at heart want Jammy Dodgers

a plain Digestive
is strictly for the restive
and not suggestive
of anything festive

Similarly Garibaldis
are for the oldies
as only old fogies
can be force fed a sandwich of bogies

Morning Coffee are easy to debunk
being impossible to dunk
An Arrowroot bicky
can also be tricky

Abbey Crunch or Bourbon Creams
are not the munch of my dreams
I'd sooner walk on hot coals bare foot
than eat Fig Rolls or a Ginger Nut

and I'd sooner be aborted
than touch Teatime Assorted

yet I can eat Chocolate Hobnobs
no probs

EURO VEGAS

Whilst neighbours on TV
replace those in the community

local and national teams
fight for our honour, glory and dreams
on our behalf, with no effort spent
comics reveal our dissent

individual within the brood
pop music captures our common mood

soundbites of art and poetry
satisfy our hunger for creativity
on demand
like a pot noodle, or a one night stand

self help teachers
we empathise like leeches

labour saving now obsolete
we need a new breed
of time consuming devices

it seems we've replaced the meat of life
with perpetual escape
and eat only the spices

OPEN GRAVES

I saw my life on a library shelf today
tucked somewhere in between Milton and Wilfred Owen
A very thin life it looked
A slim volume
A shallow grave
exhumed only twice
Easily missed
but for the lack of dust, as yet

I worked my way backwards
Meredith, Marlow, MacDiarmid
These were lives to fill volumes
like head stones
memorials
mausoleums
shaming my paupers grave

Standing back my life is lost
in the two dimensional

At a distance
very few individuals are discernable

Shakespeare
    now there was a substantial life
growing with each new century

Byron, Keats and Shelley
    often found together
a bond of over 15 decades

In time
    with lack of space
making way for a new generation
    my life displaced
        may well fall open on this page
a page as thin as any death certificate

THE CHURCH OF ENGLAND RIOTS

The Church of England is in uproar
Passions unleashed as never before
at last, closet churchgoers stand up proudly
shrugging their shoulders and tutting loudly

Stars on Sunday broadcasts a warning
news of the riots and a coffee morning

Thora Hird rallies the troops
and puts out bowls of hula hoops

The WI are mobilised
and immediately bake enough supplies
of cup cakes and mince pies
to cater for all the bring and buys

The Masonic lodges are drafted
to serve the Lord above us
selling crucifixes, hand crafted
and home made cushion covers

The Archbishop of Canterbury is forced to sigh
the Queen raises a brow over her left eye

such is the need to emote
Even Harry Secombe hits a bum note

Princess Di smiles, though coyly
and Mary Whitehouse spills tea, on her best doyly

HYMN OF THE MADONNA'S HYMEN

There's nothing esoteric
about the holiest of relics
both scientists and clerics agree

though the inhibited regale
the glory of the Grail doth pale
aside this symbol of female chastity

as do Christ's five foreskins
brought back from the crusades
the crown of thorns
and the centurion's blade

the cross and the bloodstained nails
even The shroud of Turin fails
to grace the final blasphemy

The Madonna's hymen
once examined for semen
and traces of the holy ghost
by faithless men in clean white coats

in some laboratory enshrined
labelled for DNA,
will sit
upon the shelf

Until mankind
can find a way
to clone from it,
God himself

AN ENGLISHMAN IN NEW YORK

I'd like to see Beadle in the USA
he wouldn't last a single day
he'd play just one joke
on an American bloke
and they'd blow the fucker away

WORLD TRADE CENTRE

Oh twin towers of the trade centre
what a spectacular view
from the 108th floor of number one
you can see building number two

CHELSEA HOTEL

As a tribute to Dylan Thomas
I got pissed at the Chelsea Hotel
and though the food was delicious
as a tribute to Sid Vicious
I threw up over the doorman as well

LINCOLN MEMORIAL

In Washington doth Lincoln sit
seemingly free of starling shit
If he was sat on Manhattan
his head would get shat on
unless he kept his hat on a bit

THE NEARLY FAMOUS

Reincarnation's not been kind to me
I'm history's greatest back seat driver
I've never quite fulfilled my destiny
I'm about as famous as Lord Godiva

I used to scrump apples from Isaac Newton
I was usher at the Tower of Babel
I tried to sell Rip Van Winkle a futon
I was head of Catherine the Great's stable

I dry cleaned Sir Walter Raleigh's cape
I was Samson's regular barber
I lost at bowls to Sir Francis Drake
I was the look out at Pearl Harbour

I was Ivan the Terrible's court jester
I gave Lord Wellington the boot
I was Socrates' food tester
I rented the deck chair to King Canute

I was city architect for Jericho
I was Odysseus' map reader
I was a music teacher to Nero
I was Barabbas' cheer leader

I've never quite made it in any of my lives
My fame never really got going
I was the bridesmaid to all Henry the Eighth's wives
and now I'm David Owen

JESUS FLIES BUSINESS CLASS

On the airplane I saw Robert Powell
Him who once played Jesus
So you'd think we'd be blessed with food less foul
Than just clammy ham and cheeses

SAGRADA FAMILIA (the Sacred Family)

Having spent twenty years or more
building a cathedral for the poor
I wonder if Gaudi said 'Damn'
when he was run over by a tram

He left behind the world's largest folly
and a decorative effect
on the wheels of the trolley

COLUMBUS THOUGHT THE WORLD NOT IN FACT ROUND BUT PEAR SHAPED

In 1492
Columbus sailed the ocean blue
It diminishes not his bravado
he envisaged the world as an avocado

THE UNCOMMON TOUCH

If life imitated art
I would write a poem called
If life imitated art
and this would be its start

And I would read it out at a performance
pretending it to be satirical
and just a poetic device
but courting disaster
my desperation like a half rhyme
I would try to disguise
hoping that fate
could so easily be mastered

During the poem
a woman I have never spoken to before
would recognise the desperation in my voice
as her own
she may or may not be attractive
but when she approaches me after the show
I am captivated by her presence
We talk casually passing the moments
but there is a hesitation born through longing
and all distractions blur from vision

Feigning the context of coincidence
we arrange to meet up the next day
It is sunny
and there is no awkwardness in our greeting
as twenty years melt away
we can still remember each shortened breath of this day
and all distractions blur from vision
but

And this is the but of a cynic
life will only imitate art tonight
if the poem I write will be met
with a degree of embarrassed fidgeting
and murmurs of 'self indulgent and love sick'
degenerating into general confusion
when it fails to end with a display of wit
and maybe even annoyance by some
who'd not really paid to see this kind of stuff
and later after the fact
people will avoid eye contact
especially those that recognise desperation
especially those that recognise their own desperation
and I will go home
and I will think up another poem
to help break through these barriers, trying
to achieve the control in art
that is impossible in life
knowing that I
would give away all my writing, if life
imitated art and I could have put
a full stop to this poem
before the word . . . but

TEN WAYS TO END A RELATIONSHIP (After Adrian Mitchell)

1. PATRIOTIC
   I've got to dedicate myself to work of national importance

2. SNOBBISH
   Your time allocation has expired

3. OVERWEENING
   You are too fine a human to be held back by constraints

4. PIOUS
   I shall pray you find happiness elsewhere

5. MELODRAMATIC
   I'll kill myself rather than go through this torture any longer

6. PATHETIC
   I'm not worthy of love. I can't stand anyone to see me like this

7. DEFENSIVE
   I don't have to give reasons

8. SINISTER
   I've been sleepwalking with a bread knife lately

9. LECHEROUS
   I want to fuck your best friend

10. PHILOSOPHICAL
    Well were we really going out anyway?

BEYOND MATHEMATICS

How much do I love thee
let me calculate the ways

Take the number of kisses
on the bottom of my letters
times
by the phone calls on your answering machine

Then add
warm bodies on winter nights
holding hands along the beach
and the moment you first thought of

Divide by
the forgotten anniversaries
the turning of a key in silence
and the emptiness of a meal for one

And what are you left with?

WHY I'M AGAINST CHRISTMAS, NEW YEAR, BIRTHDAYS AND WEEKENDS

I'm against the prescription of placebo on a mass scale.

I'm against the misconception that jollity, jubilation and generosity of spirit can be determined by timetable.

I'm against the surrender of all individuality and free will to a contrived agenda.

I'm against imposing a false time limitation on perceived fulfilment. (You may as well try to enforce a 10 second orgasm).

I'm against peer pressure to emulate an idealised role model.

I'm against all moral group pressure and forced obligation to suppress natural variations in temperament. I'm against any corset on the emotions, emotional fascism and institutionalised social blackmail.

I'm against the bland numbness of uniformity.

I'm against denying the complexity of the human spirit, the allure of originality and the unique nature of each human personality.

I'm against the false promise that such moments are of some universal significance or in some way representative or emblematic of some longer set period. I'm against the inevitable repercussions of disappointment and feelings of inadequacy inherently incurred

I'm against the arrogance of those converted to the culture of the calendar that all must bow to this ritual or be chastised as in some way lacking.

DB16

It's hard to die a hermit at Christmas
social conscience won't permit this

Still there's 364 other days to go
and from Boxing Day you can die alone

Only discovered when the neighbours tell
of a funny smell

Or of curtains that never move
of the constant sound of BBC Two

Of cobwebs forming in the window
of a pathway with untrodden snow

Of a washing line with the same grey socks
or of final reminders choking the letterbox

Of an infuriating record on constant replay
singing
'I wish it could be Christmas everyday'
'I wish it could be Christmas everyday'
'I wish it could be Christmas everyday'
'I wish it could be Christmas everyday'
'I wish it could be Christmas everyday'
'I wish it could be Christmas everyday'

IN DEFENCE OF THE MOUSTACHE

It's unfair to sneer at selective facial hair
though it's hard to appear unassuming
with temperance towards near nasal grooming
but an untended upper lip follicle
is not inherently symbolical of anything diabolical.

OK Hitler was a fascist
and also a noted tashist
Stalin too was without dispute a
vicious persecutor
hirsute to boot below the hooter.

However though the tash on Hitler was littler
still Adolf did rate a greater dictator
proving the fallacy of this indicator

Mussolini was also rotten
but his top lip was as smooth as a babies' bottom.

Nixon was bad though he had no
more than a five o'clock shadow
ipsofacto QED, not bec'us' he
had a mussy.

For it is writ that it is craven
to mock the partially shaven.

Though I wonder if the Bible
would have so many devotees
if the disciples
had all had goatees.

You can go from Ian Botham to Desperate Dan
and it's easy to spot who's not
a full blooded fan of Victor Kayam.

If Jesus returns
will he sport Elvis sideburns.

THE ENCHANTMENT OF PERSONALITY

In the original version
there were no real pirates and no hook
not in the physical sense
only the ominous ticking of a clock.

And at the beginning of the story
Peter was just an ordinary boy
who living in a world without fairies
had become his own shadow.

And it was he himself
who was trapped in the window.

Funny how tales change in the telling.

It was Wendy who was the heroine.

She
it was
that saved him.

She was the one who was magical
and when she giggled
as she often did
it was like the tinkling of a bell.

This was her gift that could make spirits fly.

A gift that could free lost children
trapped in their grown up clothes
and their responsible frowns.

You see the original version
was not a fairy story at all
but a love story
for those that believe in such things.

THE ADVANTAGES OF HAVING YOUR OWN HAND AS A SEXUAL PARTNER

1. Your partner is almost always available, except when driving or playing most musical instruments.

2. Your partner is never not-in-the-mood or needs persuading, cajoling, bribery or blackmail and is only ever as sleepy as you.

3. Foreplay is optional. Afterplay redundant.

4. There is no fear of sexually transmitted disease although it is advisable to be careful to wash thoroughly if recently using you hand to ease bodily strains by the application of Deep Heat.

5. There is no need for contraception. No disruptive trips to the bathroom or sudden panics about forgetfulness.

6. You don't have to worry whether you partner is enjoying the event as much as you or is disappointerd, uninspired or simply appalled by your performance.

7. You have total control of the activity and can vary each aspect according to whim.

8. You don't have to be in any way desirable, or make any concessions to appearance, hygiene, temperament or compatability.

9. Depending on your imagination you can fantasize you are with any partner of your choice. Of course this you can do when having sex with a real partner but seldom without a modicum of guilt and always with the danger of letting the wrong name slip out.

10. Although never as spiritually fulfilling as good sex with a real partner, sexual tension is released, leaving you relaxed, less irritable, less aggressive and with only half the usual mess.

BLINKING

1. I'm listening to the barber through a mirror
   conversing like a photocopier
   selling minor revelations of a personal nature.

2. Underground people
   are hanging from the ceiling like piglets from a sow
   whilst biorythms linked into the Dow Jones take a bow.

3. Somewhere without question
   lovers are praying to the pace of a botanical garden.

4. The man in the chair next
   refracts a glib eye over a woman's breast.

   He says I said you said she said they said
   This is the relativity of Franken Truth
   like 4 photos in a foto booth.

SHE HAS GIVEN OF HERSELF

She has given herself to the majesty of clouds
to twilight
and the face of the moon dying on the horizon.

She has given herself to the seasons
to the dreams of childhood
and to that which she can heal with her own hands.

She has given herself to the storm from open sea
to the silence of a cold bed
and to the flight of the highest wing across the glare.

If by chance she should see God
she would stare him full in the face
and would never be the first to look away.

SOCKS APPEAL

Some people like leather socks
or fish net socks
glittery or spangly socks
Some people don't like socks at all
Some people wear socks out of duty
or convention
Some people wear socks for show
me
I like warm socks
soft to the touch
that cushion you from the coldest of floors
and hold you gently
spreading a glow through your whole body
You can feel at home
and secure anywhere in warm socks
and
I get the feeling
nothing bad could
ever happen in the warmest of socks
the sort
you never want to take off

DEMOTING CUPID TO A CHAT SHOW HOST

I'm having to be polite
with someone whose nipples I licked
less than seven days since
Someone who's craving
hung so vulnerable on my fingertips.

It's a strange courage
that sees flight as dignity.

She is talking to me now in the langauage of social workers
She is talking to me with the demeanour
of a breakfast TV presenter.

Offering fragments of explanation
like corners from some complicated jigsaw.

Desperately earning the right to be deserving.

She's cramming for judgment day
afraid of her own breathing
preferring neon to candle
cartoon to character.

Waving at the window
as if to wipe an image from the glass.

When a child falls
there's a moment when
it doesn't know whether to laugh or cry.

It seems at the narrowest junctions
my future sits before me
purposely waiting for the lights to change
then
indicates

against the oncoming traffic.

THE CORNER OF SACKVILLE STREET

Those that solicit
illicit kisses
on the corner of Sackville Street

They too cast silver
to enlist wishes
from the well of tears
of a life incomplete

They too were once children
with promises
tender beneath their feet

All comfort is sacred
to those lost in the night

Passion sees no morality
only desire

Passion sees no morality
only desire

All comfort is sacred
to those lost in the night

ON STEPPING OUT THE DOOR ALL PAST AUTUMNS INHALED

I wish I'd never before written a poem

I wish poetry itself had never even been conceived
that I could bring you a gift
unseen before God and the angels
like the formation of the very first star
or the first new born child on Earth
but this is not to be
Yet there is beauty in the formation of all new stars
though there be a million in the universe
and isn't each child that is born as precious as the first?
So I write this poem for you
in this way
because of poems I have written before.
For even if I destroyed all my past attempts at poetry
It would be like trying to unlearn a language
or trying to forget the mechanics of walking
It is futile to romanticise naivety and deny art and evolution
My first clumsy affairs were simple couplets
juvenilia, full of basic mistakes
Later efforts showed promise but lacked true inspiration.
Limericks with the ambitions of a sonnet
Once or twice favourable development
was spoilt by an untimely ending or
the breakdown of the sense of rhyme
It seems there are very few poems around these days that endure
What I would really like to write is an epic,
an all time classic, a magnum opus,
a life's work to be left unfinished,
not the first or the last poem ever written but
a poem that would inspire all future generations
a poem that would outshine the brightest of stars
adorn the heavens and
leave even God and the angels breathless

This is the poem I would write for you

THE BINARY CODE OF EXISTENCE

You can either
be asleep or awake
talk or be silent
move or be still
eat or go hungry
drink or thirst
be alone or with company
go out or stay in
live or die
be asleep or awake
talk or be silent
move or be still
eat or go hungry
drink or thirst
be alone or with company
go out or stay in
live or die
be asleep or awake
talk or be silent
move or be still
eat or go hungry
drink or thirst
be alone or with company
go out or stay in
live or die
be asleep or awake
talk or be silent
move or be still
eat or go hungry
drink or thirst
be alone or with company
go out or stay in
live or die
be asleep or awake

EARLOBES

Pendulous understated decoration
Ripe for perforation
Why your creation
You superfluous elongation

Utterly dispensable
Your evolution nonsensical
Natural selection
Seems to have overlooked correction
Of your unwarranted projection

Is your lack of function
Divine injuction
God's grin
At Darwin
Making the origin
Of the species
Akin to a load of faeces

Oh seductive appendage
Non productive excess baggage

Have you purpose
Or are you just fleshy surplus
An etc.
Without raison d'etre

Erroneous or purely erogenous
Is there and answer to your dodgyness

Heaven sent or
Hellish bent
Oh cherished embellishment

I have no quibble
Only a desire to nibble
As you incite the cannibal

TRUST ME I'M A POET

Trust me
I'm a poet
  refining
    redefining
      revising
My business is Truth PLC

  enhancing
      enriching
            elaborating
Truth is my raw material
  My vocation
  My deity
  My mistress

      like a deft magician
    manipulating the imagery
correcting
correlating
concealing
I reveal the corruption of truth in tantalising
glimpses

  evoking the senses
     managing the facts
editing and selecting the words in my care
      omitting the irrelevant
        on your behalf

Trust me
I'm a poet
A doctor of truth

TOMORROW'S WORMS

Born
  without
    backbones
        they ooze
        from their
            holes
              they are
            processors
          of sewage
            a linear
              arse machine
                    two faced
                      they digest
                          and excrete
                              they're
                                proof
                          you are
                      what you eat
                  a cannibal
                  realisation
                  of reincar-
                      nation
                      experts
                  deem them
                  necessary
                    for more
                    than just
                        easy quarry
                          bad weather
                              brings them
                                  to the
                                      surface
                                        if you
                                        cut them
                                        in two
                                      do it
                                      length
                                      ways

CHAPEL OF THE METAL SHROUD

I stand before you as faith
in accuracy and a system man made

in distance and the white line
in direction and the painted sign

in measurement and ordained barriers
in technology and the road builders

in evolution and the mechanic's skill
in instinct and the common will

in order over the unkown
in yourself and those close to

in the motives of strangers
in society and human behaviour

FOSSILS ON COMPUTER

It is impossible to stand perfectly still
for any sustained length of time
muscles tire and strain
even the most determined are beaten
Permanence itself is a temporary illusion

Flowers bloom and wither
and new shoots emerge in their place
not the exact same petals
but no less beautiful

The weather changes hour to hour
day to day, season to season
and rain falls
never the exact same droplets
but no less fluid

There is nothing since creation
unchanged
stars disperse and reform
distances lengthen
the universe is reborn each instant
but is no less miraculous

RECOILING FROM THE ANTICLIMAX

I have seen disappointment
in eyes
       like undertakers
            sizing up my future
in limp hands shakes
            and blank glances at wristwatches
in the tactical retreat to the toilet
in forced smiles and edgy non specific answers
in the shifting of focus
in conversations that talk around or over,
                  sometimes even through
in the contortions of cocktail diplomacy

in the appointment remembered
in the sudden relapse
in the unexpected duty
in the body language of the dispassionate
in those with the ease to mingle

and as always
      I am left with the Awk
ward
                ness

knowing that any gesture I make
any fight
any sacrifice

will be
a disappointment

BOOKS BY HENRY NORMAL NOW IN PRINT –

From:
A..K. DISTRIBUTION,
22 LUTTON PLACE,
EH8 9PE
TEL:/FAX: 031 6671507

A MORE INTIMATE FAME
A5 Book, 120 pages, glossy cover, bound.
Price £6.60 (inc. p&p).

THE DREAM TICKET (Second Edition)
A5 Booklet, 52 pages, glossy cover, bound.
Price £5.40 (inc. p&p).

THE FIFTEENTH OF FEBRUARY (Second Edition)
A5 Booklet, 52 pages, glossy cover, bound.
Price £5.40 (inc. p&p).

THE THIRD PERSON
A5 Booklet, 56 pages, glossy cover, bound.
Price £5.40 (inc. p&p).

Some Recent Titles from AK Press

ECSTATIC INCISIONS: THE COLLAGES OF FREDDIE BAER by Freddie Baer, preface by Peter Lamborn Wilson; ISBN 1 873176 60 0; 80 pages, a three color cover, perfect bound 8 1/2 x 11; £7.95. This is Freddie Baer's first collection of collage work; over the last decade her illustrations have appeared on numerous magazine covers, posters, t-shirts, and album sleeves. Includes collaborations with Hakim Bey, T. Fulano, Jason Keehn, and David Watson.

SOME RECENT ATTACKS: ESSAYS CULTURAL AND POLITICAL - by James Kelman; ISBN 1 873176 80 5; 96pp; £4.50. In this collection, Kelman directs his linguistic craftsmanship and scathing humor at targets ranging from "private profit and public loss" to the "endemic racism, class bias and general elitism at the English end of the Anglo-American literary tradition."

INNA LIVERPOOL - by Benjamin Zephaniah; ISBN 1 873176 75 9; 24pp; £1.95. A selection of poems representing a small portion of Zephaniah's work as Poet/Writer in Residence with the Africa Arts Collective in 1988/89.

ON THE MASS BOMBING OF IRAQ AND KUWAIT, COMMONLY KNOWN AS THE "GULF WAR" - by Tom Leonard; ISBN 1 873176252; 24pp; £1.95. Written as the 'allies' perpetrated the mass execution of the Iraqi people, On the Mass Bombing ... exposes the hypocrisy and deceit of politicians and the military, and the media's complicity, in a concerted attempt at the wholesale destruction of a country, its people and infrastructure.

THE ASSAULT ON CULTURE: UTOPIAN CURRENTS FROM LETTRISME TO CLASS WAR - by Stewart Home; ISBN 1 873176 30 9; 128pp two color cover perfect bound 5 1/2 x 8 1/2; £5.95. "A straightforward account of the vanguards that followed Surrealism: Fluxus, Lettrisme, Neoism, and other even more obscure." *Village Voice.*

AK Press publishes, distributes to the trade, and retails mail order a wide variety of radical literature. For our latest catalog featuring these and several thousand other titles, please send a large self-addressed, stamped envelope to:

AK Press	AK Press
22 Lutton Place	P.O. Box 40682
Edinburgh, Scotland	San Francisco, CA
EH8 9PE, Great Britain	94140-0682 U.S.A.